ACHIEVING ABUNDANCE in life

SUCCESS BLUEPRINT

ISBN-13:978-1719066082

ISBN-10:1719066086

LEGAL NOTICE

Not All References to Economy and Conditions Have Been Updated from Original Writing. We Think That You'll Agree That the Messages Contained in This Book Are Timeless.

While Efforts Have Been Made to Verify Information Contained in This Publication, Neither the Authors nor The Publisher Will Assume Any Responsibility for Errors, Inaccuracies, Or Omissions Contained in This Book.

While This Publication Is Chock-Full of Useful and Practical Information, It Is Not Intended For Legal or Accounting Advice. All Readers Are Advised to Seek Competent Lawyers and Accountants Who Follow Laws and Regulations That May Apply to Specific Situations.

The Reader of This Publication Assumes All Responsibility for Any Information They May Use from This Publication. The Author and Publisher Assume No Responsibility or Are Not Liable for Any Actions Of the Reader of This Publication.

Table of Contents

PREFACE

The cover of this book has significant meaning to the authors. Neither of us comes from families that are particularly wealthy. We were both raised to have stellar work ethic and a strong sense of self. When we met, we clashed. Boy did we clash. However, beneath the clashes there was mutual respect and admiration for what the other had to offer. We both chose to foster that respect and admiration. Over time we became best of friends. We both have a strong desire to give to the world and share the abundance we have found in living what most people would consider ordinary lives. While we both started in different places in life we both feel like we have moved from the desert of scarcity, represented on the left side of the cover, to the lush green life where the river of Abundance flows daily, this is represented on the right side of the cover.

Notice, as the river feeds the life along the banks, the banks provide the river a path to flow. Each gives life to the other. This is how abundance and the partnership between the authors work. When we work together we feed each other's abundance and creativity. This has let us create a partnership, that we would like to share with the world. The sharing starts here and now with this book.

CHAPTER 1
INTRODUCTION

Humans are 3-dimensional beings. This is not obvious to everyone; in fact, most people have never considered that they are 3-dimensional. Most of those who have considered it fail to truly believe that the second and third dimensions can have an overwhelming effect on their lives. These people spend their lives without contemplating these two dimensions and if they do consider them, it is only in a vague and thoughtless manner. They live their lives dwelling on only the physical aspects. They believe that only the physical nature of life matters.

*In reality, there is **more**, so much **more** that it is difficult to comprehend.*

What are the dimensions? One is the physical presence we call our body. The second is our mind where our thoughts are created and the third is our soul or spiritual being. The combination of the mind and the soul are the most powerful gifts we own. When combined, they allow us to have and be what we desire most in life. Once merged, they produce a power that can move mountains! Learn to move the mountains that block you from having an abundant joy-filled life. You can choose to live an abundant life, or you can choose to keep plodding along wondering why you aren't gaining the results you want.

Open your mind and body merge the three dimensions and begin creating you, who you want to be and the life you want to live. Meditation is a great way to start. It teaches you to focus your mind and while you are in a meditative state you can allow thoughts to enter that may not come when your mind is tied up in work, home and family. Allow your thoughts to flow freely. Imagine what and where you want to be in life. This is where it all begins. If you don't meditate start taking some time out daily to relax and think about abundance and what you want.

Some people scoff at the idea that abundance can be created; they mock the very idea. They believe that success is for others and that ordinary people cannot have it all. They will tell you that abundant living is for others and that there is no use in trying to create a better life for yourself. There are others who casually believe that the 2nd and 3rd dimensions can help create an abundant life; however, they allow the scoffing of others to silence those beliefs, thus stifling their ability to create and live the life they want to enjoy. Don't let the scoffers hold you back! Don't argue with those who scoff. It just wastes your valuable energy. You can tell them of your thoughts and beliefs about abundant living but arguing with someone over abundance flies directly in the face of what abundant living is not about. You can't force someone else into an abundant life.

Learn all you can about abundance and see what it does for you. Those who scoff will notice the changes and ask about them, or they will continue to live a life of scarcity. Don't let their life choices affect yours. Your journey is *yours* to make. You can love and appreciate them even if they choose not to take your path. If they can't love and appreciate that you choose differently then perhaps you don't need their negativity in your life. Sometimes finding the path to abundance means making life choices that are hard but lead to better living. Only you can decide for you. There have been many people in our lives, including family members who have discouraged the pursuit of abundant living. On the other hand there have been others who have started us on the path and continually encouraged us. Some of it was intentional and some was unintentional.

Let me tell you about my friend and his parent's unintentional teachings about abundance.

He is a man who started his young life working in a café that his parents owned. He describes himself as the fat little kid who did all of the menial labor in the café. As he grew he would ask for things and his parents told him to get the things he wanted he needed to work for the money to buy them. So, he started himself a lawn mowing business. The business grew, and he hired his friends. Later in life he had a window washing business that did relatively well. This man could have been bitter at his parents for making him work. He could have pouted and refused to do the chores assigned to him. He could have blamed his parents and hated them for making him earn his way. He didn't instead he chose to learn from the experiences. He learned that by thinking he could create opportunities to make money and with that money he could obtain the things he desired in life. This set him up for future success and started him on his quest for abundant living. It is not too late for you to make the same choice.

Since you are reading this, we assume you are looking for a change in your life. If so, **now is the time** to realize that **it is** possible to have a better life. It's never too late to change your beliefs. One of our partners is in their 50's. She is finding abundance every day. She came to the learning and beliefs later in life but she's not letting age hold her back. She has always had a giving nature but now she is learning to find opportunities and give in better ways. She has always believed in the mind, body spirit connection but thought that it was only for others. She is learning that it applies to her too. Her first experiment in this realm was when she was searching for "the right" dress for her son's wedding. She found the perfect dress, just not in her size of course. She had all but given up hope when her sister said, "Visualize walking into the next store, walking up to the rack and finding that exact dress hanging there in your size." She laughed and agreed to do it. They spent 10 minutes or so talking and visualizing before choosing the next store to visit. Guess what?! They chose a store and when she walked in, found the rack with her size, and there, hanging on that rack, was THE DRESS in THE EXACT SIZE. Did this change her thinking and life overnight? Sad to say NO. It has taken several more years and exercises like this for her to start achieving the life she wants. However, that experience was a turning point.

Our group is made up of ordinary people with extraordinary beliefs that we want to share with you. We believe that the more you work on your 3 dimensions, the more you learn, the more you grow and the more you give to others and the universe, the more you receive and achieve.

There are many religions in the world and all of them have several teachings in common. Abundance is one of the common teachings. The bible states, "Cast your breads upon the waters and it will return to you ten-fold." To obtain abundance you have to believe that there is more to life than just material things. There is more to being human than the physical skin, meat and bones of your body. We see the physical world with the eye but there is more to it. There is the unseen world of spirit and mind and it influences your total being. If you allow it to influence you, you can influence it in return. Life is what you create; it begins in your mind.

Think and reflect deeply on the following:

All the modern wonders we enjoy today were created in someone's mind before they became a physical reality. Your mind is where achieving abundance begins.

Take a moment to reflect how this has already worked in your life. First, by making a conscious effort to make it clear in your "Mind" you may receive it. If you struggle with this right now don't be discouraged. We get into much--- more in-depth details later on in the next chapters.

The Fundamentals

We all have an inner world that extends far beyond what the naked eye can see. In that inner world, there is an abundance of wealth, power, and resources. This inner world gives you the freedom to live your life fully. You can choose to live large or small. You choose the way you want to live. Maybe you haven't ever thought about this world or maybe you've not been introduced to this world. Don't feel left out! A lot of people don't know about this inner world and some of those who do know won't engage in it because it's not popular; they are embarrassed to embrace a new way of thinking.

It doesn't matter which group you fall into: the group that does not know, or the ones that do not believe. We challenge you to consider giving new thought patterns a chance. A lot of people are doing their best to live in this world using just their eyes, ears, noses, mouths and skins. If this is how you have been living, it is understandable. It is the only thing many of us have known. But now, upon reading this, you have a chance to change the way you think and the way you live.

Realize there is more to life. The physical life is the tip of the iceberg. Your mind is the most powerful muscle in your body. Exercise it. If you want an abundant life, read and study the principles. Seek to understand. Search for learning materials, books, videos, and mentors. When you find the answers, you seek they will resonate within you. You will feel the truths they offer.

The biggest key to abundant living is understanding that your life is the result of where you focus your attention. Consider this: all of the five human senses are very important to us. But the five senses are not meant to rule our lives. It is wrong to say or believe that the five senses—hearing, seeing, tasting, smelling and touching—are the only extraordinary or powerful assets a human being owns. Each person created by God living in the universe has been given general gifts of physical senses. Some people are deformed in one or more of these senses, yet they continue to live full lives. Most do not let the missing part rule their life. They use their other senses to make up for those they don't have. We want you to start using your other senses (the mind and spirit) to help make up for what you lack.

While you are reading this, start to recognize that you have other very real and special gifts that go well beyond the physical body you possess. These gifts are: your brain, a soul and a wealth of imagination where you can create the world you want. It all begins with you and your belief.

The first step in achieving abundance in your life is to understand that it is a learned skill. In order to have abundance, you have to learn how to focus your mind and soul on what you desire and allow it to flow into your life. Many people have the belief that they are already living fully in all possible dimensions of awareness, but they aren't because they don't know how or don't choose to believe that their highest dimension or form is their spiritual/soul level. This level reaches outwards and connects to the world's energy. When connected to the energy, miraculous things begin to happen. It is just like the river on the cover of the book.

If you don't believe this, take some time to think about it and start accepting it as a truth. When you accept this truth, you will start to see changes in your life. Opening yourself to these thoughts and the flow of energy may be the hardest step you have to take. Just do it and see what happens! Try little experiments. Focus and visualize getting something you really want. Just like our partner did. Make it a little thing and believe that it can and will happen.

Accept and embrace the truth of your Second and Third dimensions, as you do you will find that you can use the energy there to create an abundant life; a life that is fuller and more enjoyable. The importance of using this level to operate at your highest potential cannot be overstated. Most of us were taught as children that the physical senses are all that life has to offer. We were wired to think in unproductive patterns. We were taught to hold ourselves back by people who held themselves back. We were told there isn't enough in this world for everybody, that only the lucky and special people could have rich full lives. Because we were taught these things, we either refuse to connect with the higher energy planes or we don't know how to connect with the higher energy planes. Connecting to the higher planes allows abundance to flow into your naturally-possessed, creative forces and energies.

"You are literally, what you perceive yourself to be."

Think about that statement and ask yourself who and what you are. What is important to you?

Who do you want to be?

Take the first steps and start focusing on a more abundant life today

CHAPTER 2
KNOWING THE MEANING OF
ABUNDANCE

What is the meaning of abundance? This is a word you hear or see often, but have you ever paused and thought about the meaning of true abundance and wealth? Do you know how abundance is reflected in your life? Are you wondering if you can experience abundance and wealth in your life? The answers to these questions can be obtained when you identify and observe what you are facing physically, spiritually, emotionally and financially. You must be able to acknowledge where you are in life before you can create the abundant life, the life you deserve. Knowing what you want is the biggest step towards abundant living. You cannot create what you want if you don't acknowledge the want or the need.

What It Means

A large number of people say they are living exceptionally well. This statement or claim is based on their intuition, cultural belief or perception about what a good life is or what living well is all about. Each person has to determine what it means to them. One of our partners describes it as, "Having a life full of unlimited amounts of happiness, wealth, prosperity, opportunities, sufficient materialistic items and spiritual energy. Living an abundant life has no stress attached because you have everything you need to live and give abundantly in all of the areas described" For another partner it is a more simplistic definition, "Having enough love and material items to share with others." We will write more about this later in the chapter. For now, start thinking about your definition.

To achieve an abundant life, you must use the unlimited resources available to everyone. Those who are totally willing to commit to using the resources find that they are able to prosper and end up finding out what the good life is all about.

You can achieve both abundance and wealth by identifying the necessary skills and abilities. You choose what you wish to experience in life. You can have an unlimited supply of what you want to experience in life and the resources to achieve them. You must begin by believing and maintaining a mindset that you can have the love, light and material things you desire. Keeping what you want at the forefront of your thoughts and activities will ensure that what you desire will manifest itself.

Let us illustrate this. One of our partners was determined to make $100,000 a year by the time he was 3o years old. He was in a store one day and saw some fake money. It occurred to him that the fake money might help him achieve his goal, so he bought it. He took it home and taped it all over his house. He put it in places where he would see all the time. This helped him focus his mind on what he desired. At the same time, he opened himself up to the universe and asked God to help him achieve his goal. He went about his days with the mindset that he also had to work hard towards his goal. He is now almost 29 years old and is making... you guessed it... $100,000+ a year. It was his mindset that allowed him to achieve this. He used his mental, spiritual and physical assets to do this. He has an intensity about abundant living that is hard to match!

It's unfortunate that a lot of people don't choose to have the right mindset. They focus on what they don't have, instead of what they do have. They focus only on why they haven't been able to achieve harmony, fulfillment and abundance in life instead of placing focus on what they can do to achieve the things they desire. Because their focus is on what they feel they lack, that is exactly what they attract, Lack. Maybe this describes who you are up until now. If it does, you should ask yourself the following questions:

Am I really achieving true abundance and happiness?

Am I fulfilling my goals in various aspects of my life?

Are my relationships wholesome, fulfilling and satisfying?

I get more than enough time to do what I love?

Do I have enough money to do what I want?

Is it financially rewarding and fulfilling?

Am I energetic, busy, and feel driven?

Do I love the work I'm doing?

If the answer to most of the questions above is _**No**_, it means you have not started to enjoy a good life. If the answers are Yes, then you are on the track to living an abundant life! As we mentioned before different people view and define abundance and wealth differently. Some people define abundance as being rich or having a lot of money. Some people define it based on their spiritual beliefs and perspectives. Abundant living is the combination of both definitions. When you achieve a balance of both, life is full and rich in ways you had never imagined.

There are people who value financial resources because they believe that these resources are a vital part of abundance and wealth in the world of today. We believe money is just a tiny percentage of true abundance. Unless all other vital aspects of your life are in line with one another, you will not be able to experience true abundance. It will always seem unattainable and impossible. Take some time now and think about where you are in life. Write down your answers to the questions above. Use the answers to define where you are already at the moment and where you need to focus your attention to get your life in harmony, so you can proceed on the road of abundant living. After you answer the questions take some time and write down your definition. What is abundance to you? If you haven't defined abundance and what it means to you then you will never have it because you don't have the picture of what it is in your mind. Make your description as detailed as possible. Create a very real picture of what it means to you. What does it feel, sound and taste like? How will you know when you have it? The next chapter will go into more detail on this so for now, just start detailing what you want. The knowledge of what you want and the information in the next chapter is like having a road map. Knowing where you are at this moment will help you determine how to get to your desired destination.

IT TAKES
21 DAYS
TO MAKE
OR BREAK
A HABIT

CHAPTER 3

KNOWING WHAT YOU LACK

When the basic aspects of your life are balanced, you will start to experience true and long-lasting spiritual and physical abundance and wealth

Human beings of all ages have questioned, doubted, and even fought the natural direction of their lives. You may be bored, romantically empty, overwhelmed with projects, depressed about your job, and/or feel trapped in relationship situations such as a bad marriage or children issues. You aren't alone. There are a large number of people who are busy using uninspiring work or other projects as a way to provide purpose for their lives. A large portion of them are not remotely satisfied or happy. They are only passing time and doing what they perceive to be essential, even though, deep down, they know it isn't what they truly want. We honor their reality and acknowledge that they are trying to achieve an abundant life. Perhaps it is the only way they know how. You may have been one of those people but now, you are beginning to think about something different. You are beginning to understand that you have the ability to create something different for yourself and those you care about. Don't stop now! Keep reading! Start Creating!

Take a Good Look

Do you have the desire to feel something more? Most of us crave that feeling of making a big difference in something or to someone somewhere. You know that feeling. You get it when you are involved in something bigger than yourself. It feels good, your endorphins kick in and give you that natural high. ***This*** is the feeling of abundant living. Some of us have only experienced it once or twice. Unconsciously, all of us have the desire to feel it on a regular basis. As you start this journey this feeling will be with you more and more. It will come as you move towards abundant living. When you bring all three of your dimensions into line and focus, it allows that feeling to be with you more often.

There is no doubt, that there are some naturally restless people who engage themselves in a lot of tasks, work and other projects. They believe in keeping themselves busily engaged with a lot of activities. They feel that this is a way to learn and discover new and fresh things. It gives them a reason to keep learning, growing and to never be in the same position at a given point in time. They are right. If they learn to consciously direct these urges, they are creating a more abundant life. These people view problems as opportunities to learn and grow. They take every advantage they can to use those opportunities. The biggest thing we can learn from these people is to look for opportunities in the good and bad times. Turn the bad times to your advantage and make them work in your favor. Make them your opportunity. Reflect deeply on the next paragraph:

There is a purpose behind the feeling of your life lacking something. *Your body, mind and heart are telling you that something is missing from your life.*

Keep in touch with your thoughts and feelings. If you start to feel empty. If you lack passion and purpose. If all the activities and projects, you engage yourself in begin to make you feel like you are on autopilot then you are moving away from abundance. As time goes by if you begin to have a feeling like you are not achieving or accomplishing anything valuable or important in life, this is your three dimensions working together to tell you that something is lacking and that you need to check where your focus is directed.

Some of the areas in which you may be experiencing emptiness include:

- Social life
- Love
- Relationships in general
- Meaningful work
- Application of skills
- Health
- Fitness
- Spirituality
- Finance

For you to be fulfilled and happy, it's important that you find your true passion in life. Learn to accept that all your life activities have meanings. Do not suppress yourself because you feel you have a lot of limitations; you need to allow yourself the freedom to adjust. Give yourself permission and allow the three dimensions to work together. Change your focus; change your life. This will let in more flexibility and let freedom flow through your life. You must open yourself up to possibilities that you have not allowed yourself to consider.

How are you spending your free time? Do you feel depressed? If you are, the feeling of worthlessness may come because you are not doing activities that are meaningful or valuable. Spend a minute reviewing how you spend your time. Are you going about life in a meaningless manner? Do you keep doing the same things over and over again? Are you sitting in front of a television blanking out for hours? Playing video games for hours on end? Do you spend hours on social media looking at posts of people who seem to have fabulous lives then comparing your life to theirs? If you feel like your life is worthless, these feelings are telling you that you are missing some important internal connections and external activities.

Truthfully, you are the obstacle that blocks happiness from your life. Why? Think of your life as a remote-controlled car. Who controls it? You! You have control of your own life. You hold the control and as the controller, you need to OWN IT. You are where you are because of your knowledge (or lack thereof) and where you choose to focus your energy. Don't blame yourself for your lack of knowledge. You've done the best you can according to your knowledge and abilities up to this point. But today, right this minute, you need to recognize that you have the power to change your lack of knowledge. Look at where you are. Identify your accomplishments and discover the things that you are lacking. With that knowledge, you will now have the ability to focus on filling the gaps in your life. You OWN your life! Now is the time to step up and accept responsibility for all you have and all you are. Own the desires of your heart. Only after you OWN IT can you start to change it and allow the abundance to flow through your life. Look for opportunities, positive energies and gifts that are sent your way daily. Learn to have a grateful heart and share the wealth you have right now. Use every resource you can to make your life better. Engage your three dimensions and strive for a positive life. Open the gates and start to see abundance flow into and throughout your life.

CHAPTER 4

ABUNDANCE: HOW IT WORKS

Are there problems with your finances? Do you think the real success you anticipated in your life is missing? If you answer yes to both of those questions you need to begin to establish a complete, strong connection and relationship with your higher self—your true self. Lock your three dimensions into one being. When that being is in place, you will be able to experience more success and abundance in your life. Your higher three-dimensional self is the true you. That three dimensional being is who you truly are, and you really are abundant in nature.

There is a relationship or connection between your higher self, successes, abundance and light that flows between you and the universe. The problem with a lot of people is that they have limited the way and/or medium through which abundance flows into their life. This happens due to several things. These things could include limiting and false beliefs, wrong perceptions, bad habits, negative momentum and so on. When you make a move to unite with your higher 3rd dimensional self, the abundance flow will become bigger and wider and allow more abundance to flow into your life.

The Path of Abundance

For a better view of the abundance energy stream, which is constantly flowing from the general universe through to your higher self, you will have to consider it as a great channel or medium that provides radiant energy completely flowing into your total life. Visualize it as a river that starts as a stream and gains momentum. Picture a flow of abundance the size of the Mississippi flowing through and around you. Picture it is bathing you in light and love continuously. Open yourself to the flow and let it fill your life with the things you desire most in life. Discard all your limiting and false beliefs and perceptions, remove the limiting thoughts and negative energies from your life. These things limit the flow of abundance into your life and serve as barriers preventing you from connecting with your real self. Open your mind and life to what God and the universe have for you. Turn those negatives into positives. In mathematics two negatives equal a positive. Remember that when you run into a trying situation. Change the way you view life and it will change the way you live it.

Increase the Flow of Success and Abundance in Life

If you take bold steps to overcome all of the bad habits, negative momentum and limiting beliefs and perceptions, you will find it gets easier to avoid the barriers that block the flow of abundance in your life. By nurturing positive momentum like harmony, joy and peace, you will be able to eliminate more negativity and strengthen the connection between you and your real self. When you improve the connection the flow increases. It is a never-ending circle. Embracing this way of thinking opens the floodgate of abundance that waits for you. Be sure to use the visualization of the river when you meditate. Hear the rush of the water, feel the turbulent stream of energy surrounding you and allow the warm light to bathe you in all the goodness it has to offer.

Your real, three-dimensional self knows your true ability and it is the means of achieving life success. As soon as the connection and reunion with your higher self is complete, you will be able to achieve your most sought-after dreams. Abundance and success are yours. It is not an easy path and it takes willingness to look at life in a different way. This different way of being will also help you to fulfill your purpose and mission in life. It will allow you to become fulfilled and live a meaningful life.

While you progress with the journey of life and discard your limiting beliefs and perceptions, you will see a completely new and changed life ahead. You will have a lot of work to do in achieving this, but if you take the right steps at the appropriate times, you will start to succeed, prosper and achieve abundance. Remember you own it. It is your choice and your decision. You are the one who decides to take the first step on the journey of a lifetime and it is you who makes the decisions that keeps you on the path.

Your present financial status is not only linked to real wealth, it is also linked to how you embrace abundance and the gratitude you have. Allowing the right feelings into your life is integral to obtaining the real riches and wealth. Connecting with your 3rd dimensional self is a key thing to becoming prosperous. Choose to reach out and make the connection. Start today you literally can't afford to wait another day!

Surround yourself with the dreamers and the doers, the believers and thinkers, but most of all, surround yourself with those who see greatness within you, even when you dont see it yourself.

CHAPTER 5

HAVING THE RIGHT MINDSET

Are you getting the idea that having the right mindset is the most crucial thing to own when attaining one's real potential and abundance in life? There are numerous mindsets, but the mindset that will get you where you want to be in life is the abundance mentality. This mentality is the complete antonym of the scarcity mentality. It is knowing there is enough in this world for everyone. It is trusting that the universe holds more than enough for all of us.

Scarcity mentality has its root from fear of not having enough. It is fear of losing. It is the fear that there are only a "few" of those things that we all desire. It is fear that there is not enough resources available for everyone. With this kind of mindset, you will live a life with the belief that your friends, lover, resources and material belongings are not enough. This leads to a sense of insecurity and feelings of deprivation.

Your Mindset

Abundance mentality is derived from positivity and confidence. With abundance mentality, you will have a strong belief that there are enough resources available to achieve what you want. You become someone who stops worrying about not having enough of everything, including money. This can only happen if you believe there is an abundance of resources, including money, in the world. You are very confident that even if you lose an opportunity, there are many other opportunities available and that they are only waiting to be discovered. In short, you never allow a failed opportunity to affect you negatively. When you have a negative experience, you turn it into a positive learning experience.

People with abundance mentality or those with the right mindset may have fears but they never let fear of difficult or challenging situations become obstacles. They believe that when things are not going as they have planned or wished, that a lot of opportunities—to achieve abundance in their life— still await them in the future.

We all have our individual or distinctive ability to exhibit and attract everything we want, at will. You must arm yourself with the right attitude and mindset. You must cultivate these attitudes and continually hold the right mindset. Remember that a good work ethic is part of this mindset.

Some personal traits that attract abundance in life are as follows:

1. Gratefulness: You should be grateful for the many things you have in your life. No matter what trials you are passing through right now, have a thankful heart and give appreciation for the little things. Being grateful for the little things attracts the bigger and better things into your life.

2. Belief: You should believe in yourself and your unique ability to create your own fate or destiny. You are a unique being. There is not another you anywhere in the universe! Believe you create your reality through your thoughts and actions. You need to know and believe in these things to unlock your inner dimensions and tap their power. Allow yourself to have abundance and success in life.

3. Take action: Many opportunities that can help you achieve your goals will come your way in several different forms. You should take action immediately on every opportunity presented to you. You should not await miracles but take the necessary steps to exploit the opportunities. Miracles happen when you seize opportunities. Remember to look at failures as an opportunity to learn and grow.

4. Be patient: *Do Not* try to force things to happen: Forcing things to happen can worsen matters. When you force your will against the universe you become upset and agitated. This blocks the flow of abundance. Things happen for a reason. If the things happening around you right now aren't what you want right now, recognize that you can turn them around because you have the inner power to do so.

There is nothing more important than creating the right mindset to achieve real abundance. Life should be joyful and happy for you. You should expect to love what you do and what you have.

Don't forget that the power to attract abundance starts within your 3-dimensional self and having the right mindset is where it all begins.

CHAPTER 6

DIFFERENTIATING BETWEEN POSITIVE AND NEGATIVE MINDSETS

A positive mindset is the focus you need to attain abundance in life, overcome adversity, realize your potentials and achieve your goals. Having a positive mindset does not mean that all negative thoughts and comments should be avoided.

Negative thoughts and feelings can help drive you to a new level of being. Use them to propel yourself forward. To do this you need to change a negative mindset into a positive mindset and stop saying or thinking negatively. Recognize that having negative emotions and thoughts are inherently human. Using emotional intelligence to recognize this fact and use the emotions to change for the better is a big step towards abundant living.

With abundant living comes understanding. You begin to understand that you are a uniquely created human being. Accept who and what you are. Because you are a human being, you are prone to mistakes, failure and imperfections and you are likely to react emotionally to whatever that happens to you in life. When you change how you think about the failures, imperfections and emotions, you truly begin to change your life.

Valuable Information

It's not a crime to have a negative mindset—it shows that you are human. There are lots of challenges and obstacles that you will face in life, and they will certainly disturb, unsettle and frighten you. Many people will have to experience struggles, frustrations and frightening situations at different stages of their life. These are the things that make a person stronger. If a person lets them, the challenges drive them towards achieving abundance in life.

Facing challenges and obstacles is hard and too many people let the challenges push them down and keep them there. We know that challenges are not fun and we need to acknowledge that it's not wrong if you feel bad when things do not go according to your expectation. Feeling disappointment and sadness is a normal, human reaction. Those who achieve an abundant life keep picking themselves up and putting themselves back into the flow of the universe. You have to be figuratively standing up before the flow can surround you.

A negative mindset has the power to mislead. When you have negative thoughts, it means you are moving the wrong direction with your life. It's unhealthy and unnatural to deny these thoughts and feelings. Acknowledge them, doing so allows you to recognize that there is something wrong. The way you perceive negative things and how you react to their effect has impact on your achievement of abundance. Your reaction lies in your hands. The way you handle things, weigh them and balance them matters a lot. Once again acknowledge them and move on. Don't worry yourself so much about these negative thoughts and feelings you are experiencing in your life that you block the flow. Let them push you towards the life you are meant to have. When you are having a bad day honor the reality of it and turn to your three dimensional self. Then move towards more positive thoughts and actions. Sometimes the best way to do this is to do something good for someone else.

Embrace the Reality and Have the Right Mindset

A real positive mindset always honors reality and does not rewrite history making things appear better than they were. You have to essentially and precisely define the things that you are dealing with and as you do address them. Sometimes a head on approach is the only way to make your life better. Minimizing or softening the reality of your life will make you handle it with lower energy than is required to overcome the struggle you are going through.

You will learn lessons from all the things that happen to you, and these lessons are helpful in navigating your way through the wonderful journey we call life. Despite the negativity of your present situation and how bad you may feel in your current situation, don't forget that that you are in charge of how you deal with the situations as they come. Use these times to learn from the lessons. These lessons are the source of the wisdom you need to create a world of abundance. Remember when you are going through a rough patch that you believe is more than you can handle, there is more good, in this world than you can possibly imagine.

Once you come out of a dark time the light is brighter than ever before. Turn inward to your three-dimensional self. Let it bring you to the life that you are meant to live.

Free yourself from negitive people.
Spend time with nice people who are smart, Driven, and Likeminded. Relationships should help you, not hurt you. Surround yourself with people who reflect the person you want to be. Choose friends who you are proud to know, people you admire, who love and respect you - people who make your day a little brighter simply by being in it. Life is too short to spend time with people who suck the happiness out of you. When you free yourself from negative people, you free yourself to be YOU - and being YOU is the only way to truly live.

CHAPTER 7

THE IMPORTANCE OF FAITH

An individual with strong faith finds much abundance and prosperity in his or her life. The faithful are more apt to recognize abundance for what it is. Taking steps that can boost and enhance your faith is important. Faith is important because it opens doors to abundance, creative power and limitless resources. It draws the flow of to you. To advance towards better living, you need to have faith in at least three things: Your God, your three-dimensional self, and in your abilities to accomplish your goals in life. Faith in a higher power, yourself and your abilities leads to great achievements. Your goals to achieve abundance in life will be very difficult without it. Every time you recognize a win be it big or small, use it to build your faith in those three things!

Faith

Faith is a positive element and not an empty fantasy. Faith is the force required to produce quantifiable things. According to Hebrews 11: 11, ***"...faith is the substance of things hoped for, the evidence of things not seen* (KJV)."**

Faith opens door to great achievements, it sees and knows the best solution. So, an individual with a strong faith will endure many things to achieve the things he or she seeks in life. All the great inventions and discoveries were made through a strong faith. There had to be a strong and real belief that what was created in thought would come to fruition.

One barrier to success and prosperity is not having faith in life, yourself, your God and purposeful living. Some people are unable to discover opportunities and possibilities within themselves. Part of this is because they have failed to establish the faith required to follow and inspire their life ambitions. What is your level of faith and how will you build upon it?

Unlock Your Inner Power by Increasing Your Faith

In the bible Book of Romans 10:17, faith is said to come from continuous hearing of the word of God. It emphasizes that faith doesn't come by hearing it once, but from hearing it over and over again. The word of God is important. Faith can be exercised in various perspectives, but without having a strong faith in God's word, you will limit yourself in life.

The essence and power of faith must be emphasized before you can accomplish and achieve. Jesus Christ said, *"According to thy faith be it unto you."* Jesus laid emphasis on faith and belief above all other actions in life. The Buddha and Mohammad have similar teachings. If you search the teachings of all faiths and you will find many are the same.

You were created by God for success, never for failure. As a matter of fact, God wants you to be prosperous and be and achieve a life filled with love and abundance. Therefore, you need to motivate yourself with positive affirmations and ensure that you strengthen your three-dimensional self. Rid yourself of doubt and give yourself every opportunity to succeed. You need strong faith to be prosperous and achieve abundance in all facets of your life.

CHAPTER 8

ATTRACTING WHAT YOU WANT IN LIFE

Everything on this earth, including humans, are a product of energy. Energy cannot be destroyed! Knowing this fact is the first step you need in order to take charge and change or shift your energy. As you do this, you will be able to attract what you want.

People attract energy. So, if your energy is positive, positive people and situations will be attracted to you. On the other hand, if your energy is negative, negative people and situations will be attracted to your life. Your focus in life attracts what you want.

If you feel that you always end up in situations you don't like, or you feel like you're not getting what you want in life, it could be because you're sending the wrong or negative energy. Right now, think about an item you would like to have. Next time you are out and about consciously look for it. Then begin to notice how often you see it. Soon you will feel like it is everywhere. Once that happens, picture yourself with it in your possession. The more often you do this the sooner it will become a reality. As you place your focus and send the request out to the universe, the universe will respond. You will find that what you requested has found its way to you. Remember to be patient. Sometimes requests are placed and forgotten by you then one day it becomes a reality! When it does remember you put in a request and show gratitude that it has been fulfilled.

How to Get What You Want in Life

Having determined that like energy attracts other like energy, you need to decide. What do you want to attract? The energy we are referring comes from your thoughts and beliefs. These thoughts and beliefs are picked up by your subconscious mind. Therefore, situations matching your thoughts and beliefs are created. Furthermore, people around you pick up your energy and it enters their subconscious minds. Even though these people are not consciously aware of your energy, they still develop the feelings of energy that surround you. Remember, if your energy is negative, negative people and situations will be attracted to you. This negative energy repels the positive people and situations from your life.

How This Works

If you nurture only the negative and worst things in your mind, if you don't believe that you can be successful, if you complain all of the time, if you always see the bad in every situation, if you discourage people and if you're a totally negative person, you will *always* create a negative energy, and you will continue to attract more negative things in life. Of course, this will result in more negative people and negative situations being attracted to your life. Just as a circle of negativity attracts so does positivity.

To change your negativity to positivity, you will need to change your perceptions about life and how you live it. Work towards eliminating all negative thoughts and beliefs. This is a hard action to take. You must focus on doing it one step at a time. Be aware of your thinking, the words you use, and the way you hold your body. When you notice you are being negative look for the positive. Start using good positive language. For example, when someone at your work or school complains that it is a bad place to be, reply with the good things being there does for you. If it is work reply, "It keeps food on my table and a roof over my head." If you hear complaints about school ask, "Where else could I get the education I'm getting here?" As you change your thoughts you will change your world and the world of those around you. Change the negatives to positives as you do, those things you truly want will begin to come to you.

Consciously choose to be around people who you feel are positive. When you do that you become more positive in return. You *need* to focus more on positive people, and situations. You *need* to believe and understand things will be fine, stop complaining about your problems and look for solutions to them. Be a problem solver not a problem finder. Become a more understanding person, accept and honor the reality of every situation and seek out opportunities to change what you don't like. Stop giving attention to your problems it feeds them and keeps them around. Seek to be around people who have positive thoughts and energies. Most of all, work at being positive and believe good things will happen.

CHAPTER 9

MERITS AND DEMERITS OF ABUNDANCE

You cannot achieve abundance free of charge. You have to work for it. One of the most wonderful things you can do for yourself is to become aware and conscious of the abundance and beauty already in your life. Your awareness of it will result in a greater level of gratitude thus raising the levels of positivity in your life. You must always think of abundance and start to make it a natural process. The more you devote to your awareness the more positive things you will find in your life. Consciousness of abundance and gratitude are closely connected. The more you have of one the more you will gain of the another.

Advantages

Abundance means plentiful and it could also be fullness. That is, fullness of the spirit and gratitude. You really need to be grateful if you are already experiencing abundance in your life. If you think, feel and express your thankfulness on a regular basis. You will find the following:

You attract better things as well as achieve more in life. You become more conscious and aware of the increased levels of abundance you are enjoying in your life. Your gratitude, chakras and energy increase and you become healthier. Your life is fuller and time is better spent.

DON'T BE AFRAID TO *dream* BIG

The Challenge

The challenge lies in thinking about more than just yourself. You need to focus and care more about the well-being and interest of others. Doing this is a way of showing gratitude for everything you have achieved in life. Celebrate being prosperous and enjoying abundance. Share the wealth. The world does have enough for us all if we focus on caring and sharing. Don't forget that self-pity, self-centeredness and selfishness end in misery. For lasting happiness and a fulfilled life, you need to care for and love other people. You will become happier when you make others happy and joyful. If you don't know how to do this find someone who does and mimic their actions until they become a natural way of being for you. When you give, you will surely get the reward. This principle of giving and receiving always remains the same everywhere, every time.

Which do you prefer? Happiness or misery; giving or self-centeredness? If you refuse to love others, you are closing the door to your spiritual happiness and darkness will start to manifest. Any success you achieve is meaningless without others to share in it. Does this mean give everything away? No, it means finding balance in all aspects of your life.

Happiness is not about having material gains or serving yourself. It is about being able to appreciate life and everything it offers. If you focus on this nothing can stop you from experiencing abundance in happiness and love.

CONCLUSION

To live an abundant life, you must learn to develop your second and third dimensions. You must learn to think abundantly. Abundance and prosperity are available for everyone to enjoy. We all have it in some measure. If you want to achieve more abundance, you must be aware and conscious about the abundance that already exists in your life. You can experience abundance every second of every day if you so choose.

Wealth or material treasure is not the starting point for abundance. It starts with dedicated action and strong faith. Abundance should be considered a state of mind because that is where it starts. Start being grateful for the things you have or enjoy in life right now. Take a minute and list the things in life you are grateful for having.

Things like:

Your family and, Friends.

The opportunity to be alive.

Your health, and wellbeing.

To have an education, and the ability to keep learning.

My Imagination, and Creativity

My eyes, to be able to read, and see colors.

Attracting people who inspire me.

My amazing ability to help others.

The ability to set and accomplish my goals.

How many can you list? Write it down and post it where you can see it often. Place it by the list of things that you desire. Let one list remind you of what you already have in your life and let the other list remind you of where you want to be!

No matter what you want in this life, be it peace of mind, contentment or abundance, you will get them. However, you will only get all of these when you become grateful and open-hearted. Let the flow fill you until you overflow with it on a daily basis. Always remember that abundance does not occur only by chance or opportunity. It also comes when you seize your day and accept all of the responsibilities needed to shape your future. You are starting to see what others have not seen and you are pursuing the vision of achieving abundance.

Remember the following list.

Before you can experience abundance in life, the first thing you have do is to identify and decide the meaning of abundance.

See yourself as someone who is already experiencing abundance. Recognize it in every way.

Give to other people in whatever way you can even if it is just a gift of time. Giving doesn't necessarily mean money.

When you start doing these things, you will start benefiting from the abundance you have brought to the life of others. This increases what you have to share.

You should be aware and thankful always for all of the abundance that surrounds you. This includes life, bright mornings, sweet voices of loved ones, and love in general. Your very breath is a gift of love from a higher power and it should never be taken for granted. Pause a minute every day and send your gratitude out to the heavens. It will return ten-fold.

Live your life in a way that ensures that you are focused on the abundance you long to achieve in life.

The way you want to be treated, the things you want to possess that will make you feel happy and contented.

You should understand that you create all these things by focusing on your wants instead of your perceived lack.
The universe will respond to your life focus. Most importantly, be grateful for everything you already possess.

When you live to give to others, you live abundantly. The art of giving is a secret of abundant living. Don't allow fear to be your obstacle to give. Before you can live abundantly, you must give abundantly. Once you achieve abundance, don't be selfish, share it with others and ensure the abundance keeps flowing. Add to the river so it keeps flowing and growing. Open your three dimensions and help others open theirs. The more people we add to the flow, the greater the flow for us all.

HELP US START A MOVEMENT

DO YOU HAVE A STORY THAT YOU WOULD LIKE TO SHARE?
WE WOULD LOVE TO TO HEAR FROM YOU!
WE WOULD LIKE TO GIVE YOU THE OPPURTUNITY TO BE FEA-
TURED IN OUR UPCOMMING BOOKS!

Send your submissions to:

Manfiest Success Blueprint

Att: Share-My-Story
2225 Great Lakes Dr, P.O. BOX #282, Dyer, IN, 46311

OR

Info@ManifestSuccessBlueprint.com

ManifestSuccessBlueprint.com

1-877-553-7326

ACHIEVING ABUNDANCE
in *life*

SUCCESS BLUEPRINT

Made in the USA
Columbia, SC
04 October 2023